The Selkie

Morgan Võ

The Song Cave

The Song Cave
www.the-song-cave.com

Design and layout by Janet Evans-Scanlon

ISBN: 979-8-9878288-4-7
Library of Congress Cataloguing-in-Publication Data has been applied for.

FIRST PRINTING

Contents

After all, it's better to be frightened than to be crushed.

—BELA LUGOSI

I

To Market

Let's steal to forget what we owe the world we know.

—BERNADETTE MAYER

The Four Corners

end of the day
the monger looks
back at his stall

in the black
plastic trough
just four fish
remain

one curled
in each corner
in a shrimp-like
decline

a whole batch arrives
skinny
dead
unappealing
cheap

one day they will be
fat
fresh
delectable
and worthy
of no
small expense

that one looks like a bottle
that one looks like a breast

that one looks like a caliper
that one looks like a crone

that one looks like an organ
that one looks like an op

that one looks like a paddle
that one looks like a palm

that one looks like a wizard
that one looks like a wick

that one looks like a y
that one looks like a yam

they laid in cosmic powder
silver foam had formed
around their pupils

dad said

summer
wouldn't be the same
if we were home

and had
to fly them out
all that way

and mom said

let's not
forget how
miracles

happen
in
the first place

go ahead!

the monger said

touch!

the monger stops the janitor
for a chat

this one's salmon
this one's tuna
this one's halibut
these are sardines

this one's cod
these are anchovies
this one's herring
this one's a mackerel

this one's Mahi-Mahi
this one's John Dory
this one's turbot
this one's black cod

this one's skipjack
this one's Arctic char
this one's red snapper
this one's a sea bream

and this one is a sea bass

the janitor squints

looks like fish to me

big push broom shuttling
scales away

Other Things Laying in an Ice Trough

a copy of lotus in a sea of fire
bottled water
burnt latex hospital gloves
a month-to-month lease
a new pair of plastic glasses
clasps
a darning stitch
a stool

a bully
two twenties
pig knuckles
a plate

they're still alive?!

the monger's wife asked

not exactly

the monger replied

it's just that they keep
eating and shitting

well why do you keep
feeding them?!

his wife asked

because they keep eating!

the monger screamed
angling back in his chair

a young couple
recently married
on vacation
in a seaside town

they visit a market
on an overcast day

across the way
a family gazes
on the spread of fish
atop a monger's stand

the baby meets
the couple's eyes
smiles

the baby steals
an anchovy
and runs across
to hand it off

the couple looks at each other
they look at the monger
who waves cheerfully
smiles
nods to the parents
chuckling
who blush

the young man reaches out
to lift the fish
by the tail
from the baby's grip

who giggles
and doddles back to
mom

the baby hovers
shy
then suddenly
slips away
and pulls another

the couple looks to the parents
they look to the monger
the baby comes again

the monger sighs
the monger grins
he waves his hand
to acquiesce

mom covers her mouth
dad slaps his knee

the young woman reaches out
to pluck the second fish
from the baby's hand

the baby races back
behind dad's legs
wrapping arms
around his knees

tsk tsk!

the monger kids

the baby takes
the parents by
the hand

walking past the young
man and woman
the baby waves

bye bye!

and the couple laughs

see you later!

when dad pivots
swiftly
to say

let's not
make
a promise

we know
we cannot
keep!

then pivots
to march swiftly
away

he clutches three in each hand

he sneers and they cower
they sneer and he howls

rose-tinted drippings
the sound of a zipper

he whispers

> manchester plays
> oxford today
>
> bloody bastards
> better win

and they cheer

a fish wrapped in newspaper
given to the baby to read

the oldest and slowest wisdoms
the baby acknowledged with a cry

shelter! she shrieked find shelter!
pressing fish to cheek

the prisoner of love continued
freshly rotting each new day

the monger hates how
seagulls circle

    birds, birds, birds!

he shakes his fists

    birds, birds every
    day!

the seagulls love how
mongers work

    fish, fish, fish!

they snap at air

    fish, fish, fish,
    fish, fish, fish,
    fish!

flying fish angel
coconut horns on its back

a tiny cretin
towed through the sky

screeching like fire birds
sweet smell of a long jetty's foam
a gout-hobbled knee

pouring
corrosively bright drops of water
so salty so dense

silent shell goes far in the distance

the monger and his wife
sitting at the table

the monger has a legal
pad and pen

he asks
and she replies

favorite word?
succor

favorite color?
champagne

favorite animal?
the crane

favorite actor?
cher

favorite season?
late spring

favorite movie?
splash

favorite novel?
the idiot

favorite phrase?
such as it is

favorite meal?
a stewed squid i had in venice

favorite memory?
flying kites from a lighthouse

favorite class in school?
there was this one class

i took on weekends
in junior high

we'd meet at a wetlands preserve
and gather soil samples

and samples of the water
to map the acidity

of the area
it held some of the last pocosins

in virginia
peaty bogs full of shrub life

mrs. cantrell
would speak like she was

telling us stories
they were stories of admiration

and of loss at the same time
of respect for

all the incredible resources
specialized habitats offer wildlife

and the greater world
pocosins are excellent carbon sinks

they help with flood control
and filter water

they can be crucial to migrating birds
because berries go uneaten there

i know i learned all kinds
of important things

when i was in school
but going out there regularly

becoming intimate with that place
and learning what made it unique

understanding what the loss
of that uniqueness would mean

was an early experience of
knowing that learning was

important to me
something i would continue to do

favorite fruit?
persimmons

favorite vegetable?
fresh scapes

favorite dessert?
chocolate cake

favorite show?
i'm not sure

the monger nods
he's writing everything down

i see i see
he says

tapping his pen on
his pad

he holds his phone
to a tiny eye

above a broken window
on the passenger side
of an old sedan
the meme reads

stay safe y'all
last night somebody
left two Dababy
tickets on my
windshield

this morning
Dababy himself
broke in
and left
four more!!!

    ha!

he cries

    stay safe!

he laughs

    haha!
    four more!

dad asked

isn't there a joke
about fish
in red lipstick?

the monger replied

of course!
it goes

a hole opened in the sky
and the sea rose to meet it

dad repeated
confused

a hole opened in the sky
the sea rose to meet it

mom said beneath her breath

a hole?
the sea?

the baby grabbed it
from the air
declaring

that's not so funny!

and the monger said

so be it

before tossing one off
to the birds

by accident or mistake
one of the fish
gets shuffled in with the cash

the monger fails to notice
a clammy white tail
poking out from his wallet

the banker takes it
she washes her hands but
she does that after
every touch

the atm passes it out

in just one week
the fish is used to pay for

an oil change
a bag of candy
a seafood platter
margarine
tickets to *Black Adam*
a discount prescription for albuterol
discount ammo
lavender-scented candles
a toll

weeks and months
and years go by

eventually
the fish gets worn in two
then taped together again

then passed back out
by a firmly held hand

dad bites

mom bites

the baby twists a spiteful face

mom says

> if it fits
> in your mouth
> it's natural!

tiny baby bites

there is a marinade
of soy sauce
dill
cumin
white and black pepper

there is a grain mix
of quinoa
cilantro
buckwheat
and wild rice

the monger and his wife were walking
barefoot on the beach

he stepped on a burr
she stepped on some dross

he stepped on a shell
she stepped on a plank

he stepped on a fry
she stepped on a frank

he stepped on a bolt
she stepped on a link

he stepped on some pop
she stepped on a bone

he stepped on a cable
she stepped on a boom

he stepped on the water
she stepped on a bill

he stepped on a corner
she stepped on a joint

he stepped on a band-aid
she stepped on a block

he stepped on a tire
she stepped on a brake

he stepped on a quarter
she stepped on a pint

he stepped on a caper
she stepped on a pit

he stepped on a washer
she stepped on a drape

he stepped on a pile
she stepped on a stave

he stepped on a shade
she stepped on a pail

he stepped on a blazer
and she on a loafer

he on a plate and
she on a braid

he on a file
and she on a slip

he on a whistle and
she on a beam

they stepped on and on
wincing and squeaking

holding their tongues
and soldiering on

out past the anchors
out past the piers

into the distance
into the darkness

into the surface
into the breakers

into the currents
into the tide

up in the details
up in the cosmos

like a new spout of oil
a spiral was guiding

waving light fingers
like a sonar they could see

that one is invisible

that one is perfectly clear

he turned
he continued
pointing
very scanty fingers

that one was over there

that one was there before!

that one never had a mouth

it sucked on krill
through its gill
just enough to stay
alive

it had hunger-induced
hallucinations
that its siblings
never had

shared memories
were sometimes remembered
differently
as though different
events but they
were definitely the same

they all communicated
by clicking tiny
bones in their jaws

the fisherman felt lucky

where a slit
should have been
there was a healthy
bit of meat

and because
it was only hanging
from the hook by
a fin wrapped
twice around

you buy two
you drive them home

late at night
you notice something stuck
inside one's chalky lip

you reach in
with finger and thumb

you reach a thin scroll
it reads

after

all

you

know

and

tibet

is

still

not

free?

for carnival
she straps a dried fish
to her groin
as her penis for
the night

he straps a wet one
from his navel
as his pussy

dangling
one looks across at the
other hanging there
swaying from their
silken belts

they go
dancing through a cobbled street
stretching for the crumpled snow

they use fish to stain the skin around their eyes

they use fish to make sequins a dark color green

they use fish to find leaks in pools

they use fish to induce labor

they use fish to send messages to people who have died

they use fish to catch birds

they use fish to oil hinges

they use fish to fertilize corn, peanuts, garlic, and wheat

David Blaine
goes to a
fish market
looking for
good sturdy
props

the monger had gone
to the local library
to see chef anthony bourdain
on his latest national
book tour

it had been an inspiring night

in his opening remarks
bourdain had said

> i've gotten
> along with
> people
> everywhere
> in this world
> and i've heard
> some amazing
> stories
>
> largely because
> i sit down
> without an agenda
> and ask
> two very
> simple
> questions
>
> what makes
> you happy?

and

what do you
like to eat?

the monger had thought
tortilla chips
fresh ceviche
and cold narragansetts
while getting stoned
with his wife
at the end of september

bourdain had said

as i think i've said
before

the presence of
livestock
or chickens
in the dining room
is often the
mark of
a good meal

the monger had tried to
imagine a cow's
head so close
to the table

so still and slow

he imagined reaching out
to pet it
and everyone's eyes
trained on his

bourdain continued

> i was there for
> the full ride
>
> how many times
> am i going to
> get to go
> to vietnam
> in my life?
>
> how many times
> am i going to
> sit down with
> a table of
> viet-cong
> war heroes
> in the middle
> of the jungle?
>
> so when they broke out
> the rice moonshine
> and everyone wanted

to do a shot with
the visiting american
i felt obliged to take
full advantage of
that magical moment

and also

he laughed

there's a competitive
urge

the monger remembered
a current events assignment
he'd had in high school
to summarize something
from the evening news

when he got his back
the teacher had written
in big red letters

THE NAM IN
VIETNAM
IS SPELLED WITH
AN 'A'
NOT AN 'O'

bourdain had said

a good line
cook never
shows up late
never calls
in sick
works through
injury
and pain

working
through pain
and injury
that counts
for a lot
with me

the monger remembered
his dream from that morning

he was back
in the kitchen at
waterman's
the first kitchen
he'd ever worked
only it was totally empty
not even the stoves
and nearly pitch dark
cold tile floors
and echoing walls

old luis was there
the tiny grill man
the monger couldn't
see his face
just his head
from behind
and his shoulders
in stiff white cloth
he looked busy
moving forward
toward the hall
the monger followed

when suddenly
luis was behind the monger
pulling him from
the neck
down to the floor
not a word or thought
just the weight
of the man's
complete control

fear took the air
from the monger's chest
as he settled onto
his knees

he looked up to where
the dark wall

met the dark ceiling
and woke in a sweat
totally confused

bourdain had asked

> what type of person
> gets to be happy?
>
> and what type of
> person
> invariably doesn't?

the monger had thought
of the janitor before
the latest janitor

it had been about
six years since
he'd been canned

the monger had thought
they might see
each other around
maybe at the bar nearby
but it hadn't happened yet

bourdain had said

i often compare
the experience
of going to tokyo
for the first time
to what eric
clapton and pete
townsend must
have gone through
the week that jimi
hendrix came to
town

you hear about it
you go see it

a window opens up
into a whole new
thing
and you think

what does this mean?

what do i have left
to say?

what do i do now?

the monger had thought back
to another talk at the library

a filmmaker
who's name
he couldn't
recall

she'd said
the plan
had always been
for her greatest
ambitions
to be held
at human scale

she'd said
on her set
everybody carries
the lights

everybody cooks
the food

everybody's tired
they set up the tents

everybody sleeps
like it's part
of the game

who can go harder?

who can turn out
the night's
deepest dream?

the monger
thought of her
every now and again
when he surfed
which

these days
with everything else
was only ever
just a few times
every year

I made one out of lead

I made one out of mirrored plexi

I made one out of video cameras

I made one out of brick

I made one out of guitar strings

I made one out of newspaper

I made one out of photos

I made one out of fish

I made one out of sugar

I made one out of paint

I made one out of novels

I made one out of soap

I made one out of rubber

I made one out of cream

I made one out of colored lights

I made one out of steam

April 30, 1975

STATEMENT

I, The Monger, plan to do a one year performance piece, to begin on April 30, 1975.

I shall seal myself in my stall, in solitary confinement inside a tray of ice measuring 6' x 3' x 2'.

I shall NOT converse, read, write, listen to the radio or watch television, until I unseal myself on April 29, 1976.

I shall have fresh fish every day.

My friend, The Janitor, will facilitate this piece by taking charge of my fish, clothing and refuse.

The Monger

The Monger

111 Hudson Street, 2nd/Fl. New York 10013

November, 1976

STATEMENT

I, THE MONGER, plan to do a one year performance piece.

I shall chuck a fish from my stall every hour on the hour for one year.

I shall immediately leave my stall, each time after I chuck the fish.

The performance shall begin on November 11, 1976 at 7 P.M. and continue until November 11, 1977 at 6 P.M.

The Monger

The Monger

111 HUDSON ST 2FL N.Y.C. 10013

April 26, 1978

STATEMENT

I, The Monger, plan to do a one year performance piece.

I shall stay OUTDOORS for one year, never go inside.

I shall not go in to my stall, a building, subway, train, car, airplane, ship, cave, tent.

I shall have a sleeping bag.

The performance shall begin on April 26, 1978 at 2 P.M. and continue until April 26, 1979 at 2 P.M.

The Monger

The Monger

New York City

February 4, 1980

STATEMENT

We, The Monger and A Fish, plan to do a one year performance.

We will stay together for one year and never be alone.

We will be in the same room at the same time, when we are inside.

We will be tied together at waist with an 8 foot rope.

We will never touch each other during the year.

The performance will begin on February 4, 1980 at 6 P.M. and continue until February 4, 1981 at 6 P.M.

A Fish

A Fish

The Monger

The Monger

111 Hudson Street, 2nd/Fl. New York 10013

February 1, 1982

STATEMENT

I, THE MONGER, plan to do a one year performance.

I █████ not sell FISH, not talk FISH, not see FISH, not smell FISH, not go to FISH stall and FISH market for one year.

I █████ just go in life.

The performance █████ begin on February 1, 1982 and continue until February 1, 1983.

The Monger

NEW YORK CITY

July 31, 1983

STATEMENT

I, The Monger, have a 13 years' plan.

I will sell FISH during this time.

I will not sell it PUBLICLY.

This plan will begin on my 36th birthday July 31, 1983

continue until my 49th birthday July 31, 1996.

The Monger

The Monger

EARTH

the monger kisses each fish goodbye

the fish kiss back with hands
across each eye

the monger's wife
is home alone
typing into the search bar

real mermaid small breasts

real mermaid long hair

real mermaid long kiss

real mermaid arched back

real mermaid drying off

real mermaid taking bath

after lunch's sandwich
the afternoon's tingly swig
of listerine

every day's a stinker
and a feeder

every day cleans and drains
closes up
and frames

lately
the monger doesn't feel
like laughing

the days he's had
the days at work
the days at home
the days in the news
the one day done with
the days ahead

the monger feels that
sunshine has lately
creased on sight

that clothing has
lately bore no
weight

that moments
have lately
stepped apart
to face away
from him

he wishes he
could concentrate
his breath
to change the air

or write a law
to sew connections
back together

the worst
is when he's just
left his stall
or walked
out the door
in the morning

when he rubs
a thumb
against his keys

when he is turning
from a counter
placing change
inside his
pocket

going from
place to
place has lately
felt like testing
an ankle
that hasn't yet
been reconciled
isn't finished
being pain

you bury one foot in
the fish book

the other foot stays stuck inside
the cloudy book

the fish book outlined
full-lipped
pokeable pages

the cloudy book blowing
heavy doling
fragile packet

one foot chops while
the other whisks

one foot gasps while
the other grays

both start to weather
both start to stew

both start to ferry
both start to flake

both start to soften
both start to rise

both books flip open
you put down another
extension in each

a knee and a hand
an eye and a ball
one hair after the other
an ear and a breast

one of each
until both halves
have been
evenly
apportioned

half starts to taper
half starts to bind

half starts to barrel
half starts to drive

half itches
half slips

half mimics
half pries

half ripens
half shortens

half eases
half hones

both halves get clammy
both halves grow prone

to pattern
to influence
to index
to price

but for the half
in the fish book
it's more like
a tug

for the half
in the cloudy book
more like a
push

a push from behind
a tug into darkness

you tumble out the
boundary of
a tawny overhead
light

I spread mine on toast

I dip mine in coffee

I coat mine in flour

I bring mine to boil

I dress mine with oil

I chill mine on ice

I whip mine for custard

I drop mine on rice

their skin is scales

8pm and lightly raining

the janitor takes a glance
around the empty grounds
before he goes

shadow here and
shadow there

shadow
over shadow

echoes
out
then echoes
back

negative space as compact cases

empty tents
the tubs overturned and
drying

flagpole silhouettes
against the gray-green sky

the janitor develops a sordid
fantasy

on his way out

he laughs and grimaces
being spun about his secret
spike

II

After Death

A Look into a Succulent's Finger

Vitality is a set of cards that must be played with cards of sickness. Like a dying trout held flat against the window, one eye on the yard in late spring, its late invasive rain. One eye on the wrist of the hand holding its neck and chest, on the wrist a corsage of succulents and frail white flowers. Each succulent makes a regular kaleidoscope of its engorged rubbery leaves, the perfect distribution of its fingers in circular time. Each flower a crumpled kleenex. Each card a business card. A look into a succulent's finger distributes a card, that falls to the ground lightly like kleenex. Beams that break through pans of sky bounce off the floor and pile up on the cards. Vitality cards are all red on the front, sickness cards all blue. But even though they're bunched up in crumples, they've landed so only the backs can be seen, and the backs are all white. One eye sees deck chairs flushed under rain. One eye delights on the complex of crumples. Each lost respiration is felt with a flower placed in a gill.

After Death

After death, the world is experienced again through old memories of a benign orthostatic (postural) hypotension and the re-balance achieved by wrapping two hands around opposing sides of a doorframe. Balance is engendered by a flexible metal bar holding up the shoulders: two tight bald heads developing ESP. Its symptomatic accompaniment bears a sudden accumulation of sanguinated dots and arrows oversaturating the visual field, to the point that light must be exhumed and/or beckoned from its low tide hiding place, while dark messages fly to and fro inside the havoc. Heaven is this excited heaviness, where clarity has no truck.

The Selkie

Monday morning, a Form of Fish Life walks into a hardware store. Guy behind the counter asks, *How can I help you?* In broken English, the FFL says, *Trash bags, bleach, plaster, tape.* Guy behind the counter says, *Coming right up.* He gathers the items, rings it up. He says, *That comes to $51.22.* The FFL hands him three twenties, takes the change, and drags the purchase out of the store.

Tuesday morning, the FFL returns. Guy behind the counter asks, *Hi again, how can I help you?* The FFL says, *Hi. Trash bags, bleach, plaster, tape.* The guy behind the counter asks, *Already? Well, no problem.* He gathers the items, rings it up. He says, *That comes to $51.22.* The FFL hands him three twenties, takes the change, and drags the purchase out of the store. Wednesday morning, same deal. For the rest of the week, the FFL comes in first thing each morning, asks for trash bags, bleach, plaster, and tape, pays with three twenties, then drags it away.

The following Monday rolls around. Guy behind the counter already has everything ready to go. The FFL walks in. Smiling, the guy behind the counter says, *All ready for you.* He pats the items. The FFL waves its fin, *Not today. Today, nails, glue, cardboard.* The guy asks, *Nails, glue, cardboard?* The FFL nods. The guy behind the counter shrugs, pushes to the side the items he'd prepared, goes to grab the nails, glue, and cardboard. He returns, rings it all up, says, *Comes to $12.61.* The FFL hands him a ten and a five, takes the change, and turns to the door. Guy behind the counter says, *Guess I won't know what to expect tomorrow.* The FFL turns, smiles, winks. *New week, new job,* it says, before dragging the stuff out to the truck.

Earth Falls into Heaven

When Earth falls into Heaven, then there'll be peace. When the floors let go of memories, and Heaven reaches out to take them up, reaches around us and our own hands and our eyes. When we reach out to grasp the air and the clouds dissipate—when the jet streams are struck by our hands and pulled to our faces. Then there'll be music as the wind struggles, the music of a desperate world against the heads of small people. When motions and forces objectify our bodies, aimlessly, guiltlessly, events without memory. When there is no weather report, and the birds have gone into separatism, then there'll be stillness, an extension of stillness that is its own form of land—a renewed chance for peace. When Earth becomes a star and enters the world of Heaven, then there'll be an emptiness that doesn't rob time in order to keep itself calm. Then there'll be another form in which to ferry peace.

III

The Selkie

think of me
I think of you
accruing
inferences
hot on the flecked
trail of past meteors
come in
I come to you
heavy with rattle
the kind of animals
you carry too

A Pillow as a Present

you are the remnants of an audio pornography
your world is a patchwork quilt of threadbare relation
which you share with your quivering life
in the center of winter

you pour relation over your life's breasts
over the banister of the balcony
into a paper cup for the neighbors
who sleep through your disaster
in truth they are as present
as a pillow soaking up the sea

you pour disaster over your own ass
to become the ashes of an echo
to complete circles in the snow
driving blood into the fingernails
and tar around the field

starlight can now bounce across
your smoothed unholy surfaces with messages
of a charred and distant past
each star it is your birthright
to place inside your daily routine

you are a catcher who would shake ill
but for the cold proliferation of sound

People Like Monsters

People want to get squished or eaten whole, and not so secretly.
People want a short distinction between life and death.

Imagine the wholesomeness of curling into a dark throat.
Being a sucker once on the street, then soaked in blood.

You learn there, listen, last; gargles leaping down your body.
Thirty seconds.

You think out loud, *I'm close, and no one's looking.*
Here's what destiny has to say in its god darkness.

Late at night

Lost at night

They left that night

They leapt at night, to scare night, their fingers curled as if attacking

They blamed night for the oneiric sorrows the early hours had
brought

They, only human, slept at night

They felt at night a sense of loss, that gave them a sense of pride
for surviving, and the fear that their emotions were not under
their control

They stole at night

Less at night

They helped at night when others slept

They felt for the light at night, sullying their walls

They flossed at night, which made them plastic beehives

They locked their doors at night

They bleated at night when they heard huge talons scraping trees

They came closer at night, their lovers and the fear of life

Sliding beneath the robe that opens to a glade of anonymous,
sparkling, translucent dots

The Break

can your strength come from being a loser?
the loser son of your idiot father (also a loser)
who comes from a country of losers living

ominously in a whole world of losers
waiting small-eyed for a break?
there won't be a break

not one second when things will
ever change
when the losers will ever win

hey
if you do find a winner
take a picture
mail it to someone who cares

I love crowds in the stratosphere
I love crowds in the sea

of dust and charge
of tactic and gas
of feedback and flicker
of military green

crowds that keep no bones no meter
crowds without below or aft
crowds that leave no odor no phone

they need elaboration, they are elaborate
they do not lack for trails of crumbs

crowds are calluses in spite of floating
above the bottom, below the sea

The Selkie

A fish will lick my fingers while I sleep deeply.
A pineapple fish will unite all places savvily combined.
A broken rose of fish drifts through clouds of baby formula, to be
berated by
A dozing sea. Burrow, ochre craniates! Crater deep below the
steam vents
At the Marianas. I am claiming antlers of the sea, my hands rein
back on sharp-edged
Antlers, and the taking of a train across the bottom in the black.
The antlers are the corraded vertebrae of
A fish train piled miles, miles high.
Adrift in clouds of scented soap, fried in corn oil, and served on
plates of empty files. One fish turns to me to tease my lack of
knowing: "The claypot is
A motor structure that links tarnished extant terms like coils of
A spring."

Notes

pg. 23
"a hole opened in the sky / and the sea rose to meet it" is from Dao Strom's *You will always be someone from somewhere else: poetry/fragments* (Ajar Press, 2018).

pg. 38-47
"A good line cook never shows up late, never calls in sick, works through injury and pain … Working through pain and injury, that counts for a lot with me," is from Anthony Bourdain's *Kitchen Confidential: Adventures in the Culinary Underbelly* (Ecco, 2007). Other quotes attributed to Bourdain were adapted from video clips featured on the @anthonybourdainfanclub IG channel.

The filmmaker referenced is Kelly Reichardt.

pg. 49-54
These pages echo the one-year works of Tehching Hsieh and Linda Montano.

Acknowledgments

Previous versions of these poems have appeared in *Changes Review*, *The Brooklyn Rail*, The Poetry Project's *Footnotes*, and the *Pathetic Literature* anthology (Grove, 2022). Thank you to the editors of these publications for giving this work encouragement, space, and context.

—

I'm glad to be part of a poetry community so wide that I don't know the bounds of it, and I may never meet you all, but your presence supports me in my insistence that poetry is crucial and inevitable, wherever life for the living of it is to be lived. Thank you forever to the Poetry Project, and particularly to my comrades these last seasons: Anna Cataldo, Kyle Dacuyan, Will Farris, Kay Gabriel, Laura Henriksen, Bianca Rae Messenger, Roberto Montes, and Nicole Wallace.

With deepest gratitude: To Ben, Alan, and Janet, for carving a place for this book in their cave. To Lena Takamori, who has helped with set design on many special occasions. To my teachers, always—for these poems especially, thank you to Vi Khi Nao (tennis coach) and John Godfrey (side gate). To Sam White, for sewing on a zipper. To Anna Gurton-Wachter and Rachel James, for being candid on air. To Taylor Shields, for the multi-directional necklace. To Saki Sato and Kirby Chen

Mages, for the mixed bag. To Vani Natarajan, for the long-running email.

To my grandparents, my mother and father, my brothers, my aunts, uncles, and cousins, thank you for the shelter of your love and playfulness, and for the textures of our dissonance.

To Nara, for animal instinct. To Bình, for coming in. To Laura, for your thrash and glance. I'll meet you three on the corner in ten.

Thank you.

OTHER TITLES FROM THE SONG CAVE:

1. *A Dark Dreambox of Another Kind* by **Alfred Starr Hamilton**
2. *My Enemies* by **Jane Gregory**
3. *Rude Woods* by **Nate Klug**
4. *Georges Braque and Others* by **Trevor Winkfield**
5. *The Living Method* by **Sara Nicholson**
6. *Splash State* by **Todd Colby**
7. *Essay Stanzas* by **Thomas Meyer**
8. *Illustrated Games of Patience* by **Ben Estes**
9. *Dark Green* by **Emily Hunt**
10. *Honest James* by **Christian Schlegel**
11. *M* by **Hannah Brooks-Motl**
12. *What the Lyric Is* by **Sara Nicholson**
13. *The Hermit* by **Lucy Ives**
14. *The Orchid Stories* by **Kenward Elmslie**
15. *Do Not Be a Gentleman When You Say Goodnight* by **Mitch Sisskind**
16. *HAIRDO* by **Rachel B. Glaser**
17. *Motor Maids across the Continent* by **Ron Padgett**
18. *Songs for Schizoid Siblings* by **Lionel Ziprin**
19. *Professionals of Hope: The Selected Writings of* **Subcomandante Marcos**
20. *Fort Not* by **Emily Skillings**
21. *Riddles, Etc.* by **Geoffrey Hilsabeck**
22. *CHARAS: The Improbable Dome Builders* by **Syeus Mottel** (Co-published with Pioneer Works)

23. *YEAH NO* by **Jane Gregory**
24. *Nioque of the Early-Spring* by **Francis Ponge**
25. *Smudgy and Lossy* by **John Myers**
26. *The Desert* by **Brandon Shimoda**
27. *Scardanelli* by **Friederike Mayröcker**
28. *The Alley of Fireflies and Other Stories* by **Raymond Roussel**
29. *CHANGES: Notes on Choreography* by **Merce Cunningham** (Co-published with the Merce Cunningham Trust)
30. *My Mother Laughs* by **Chantal Akerman**
31. *Earth* by **Hannah Brooks-Motl**
32. *Everything and Other Poems* by **Charles North**
33. *Paper Bells* by **Phan Nhiên Hạo**
34. *Photographs: Together & Alone* by **Karlheinz Weinberger**
35. *A Better Place Is Hard to Find* by **Aaron Fagan**
36. *Rough Song* by **Blanca Varela**
37. *In the Same Light: 200 Poems for Our Century From the Migrants & Exiles of the Tang Dynasty,* translated by **Wong May**
38. *On the Mesa: An Anthology of Bolinas Writing (50th Anniversary Edition)*, edited by **Ben Estes and Joel Weishaus**
39. *Listen My Friend, This Is the Dream I Dreamed Last Night* by **Cody-Rose Clevidence**
40. *Poetries* by **Georges Schehadé**
41. *Wings in Time* by **Callie Garnett**
42. *Two Murals* by **Jesús Castillo**
43. *Punks: New & Selected Poems* by **John Keene**
44. *ABC Moonlight* by **Ben Estes**

45. *Star Lake* by **Arda Collins**

46. *The Maybe-Bird* by **Jennifer Elise Foerster**

47. *Seriously Well* by **Helge Torvund**

48. *Dereliction* by **Gabrielle Octavia Rucker**

49. *Bookworm: Conversations with* **Michael Silverblatt**

50. *April* by **Sara Nicholson**

51. *Valley of the Many-Colored Grasses* by **Ronald Johnson**

52. *The Sphinx and the Milky Way: Selections from the Notebooks of* **Charles Burchfield**

53. *Telling the Truth as It Comes Up: Selected Talks & Essays 1991-2018* by **Alice Notley**

54. *Lunar Solo: Selected Poems* by **Jules Laforgue**

55. *Stranger* by **Emily Hunt**